EXPLORING WORLD CULTURES

Lebanon

By Menna Landon

Cavendish
Square

New York

Published in 2022 by Cavendish Square Publishing, LLC
29 East 21st Street, New York, NY 10010

Copyright © 2022 by Cavendish Square Publishing, LLC

First Edition

Website: cavendishsq.com

This publication represents the opinions and views of the author based on his or her personal experience, knowledge, and
research. The information in this book serves as a general guide only. The author and publisher have used their best efforts
in preparing this book and disclaim liability rising directly or indirectly from the use and application of this book.

All websites were available and accurate when this book was sent to press.

Library of Congress Cataloging-in-Publication Data

Names: Landon, Menna, author.
Title: Lebanon / Menna Landon.
Other titles: Exploring world cultures.
Description: New York : Cavendish Square Publishing, [2022] | Series:
Exploring world cultures | Includes bibliographical references and
index.
Identifiers: LCCN 2020039620 | ISBN 9781502662477 (library binding) | ISBN
9781502662453 (paperback) | ISBN 9781502662460 (set) | ISBN
9781502662484 (ebook)
Subjects: LCSH: Lebanon--Juvenile literature.
Classification: LCC DS80 .L36 2022 | DDC 956.92--dc23
LC record available at https://lccn.loc.gov/2020039620

Editor: Caitie McAneney
Copyeditor: Jill Keppeler
Designer: Rachel Rising

Some of the images in this book illustrate individuals who are models. The depictions do not imply actual situations
or events.

CPSIA compliance information: Batch #CW22CSQ: For further information contact Cavendish Square Publishing LLC,
New York, New York, at 1-877-980-4450.

Printed in the United States of America

Find us on

Contents

Introduction

Lebanon is a nation of **diverse** belief systems, foods, and **traditions**. The culture, or way of life, of Lebanon's people is very rich and **complex**.

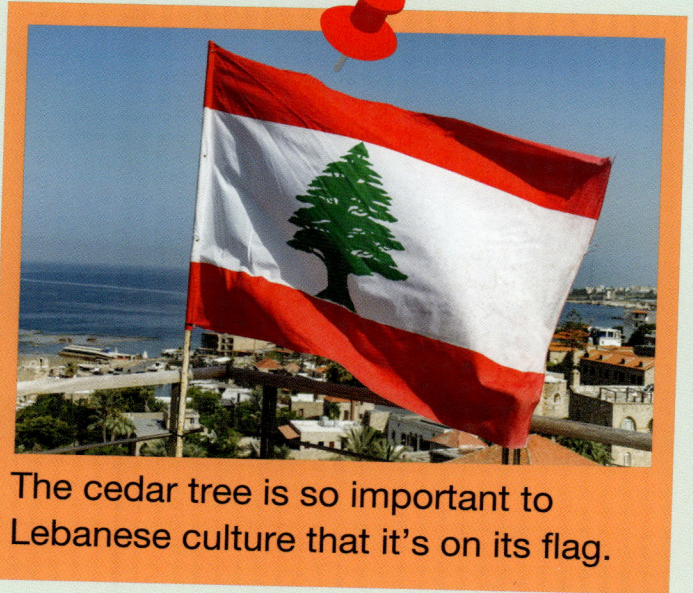

The cedar tree is so important to Lebanese culture that it's on its flag.

That's because Lebanese people come from many different backgrounds.

Lebanon is located in a part of Southwest Asia often called the Middle East. It sits on the Mediterranean Sea, with Israel to the south and Syria to the north and east. Some of the earliest settlements in the world started in today's Lebanon. Its capital city, Beirut, is one of the oldest cities in the world that people have lived in nonstop.

Lebanon is a place of old buildings and modern cities. It's a place of snow-topped mountains, cedar forests, and coastline. All these things helped create the culture that's there today.

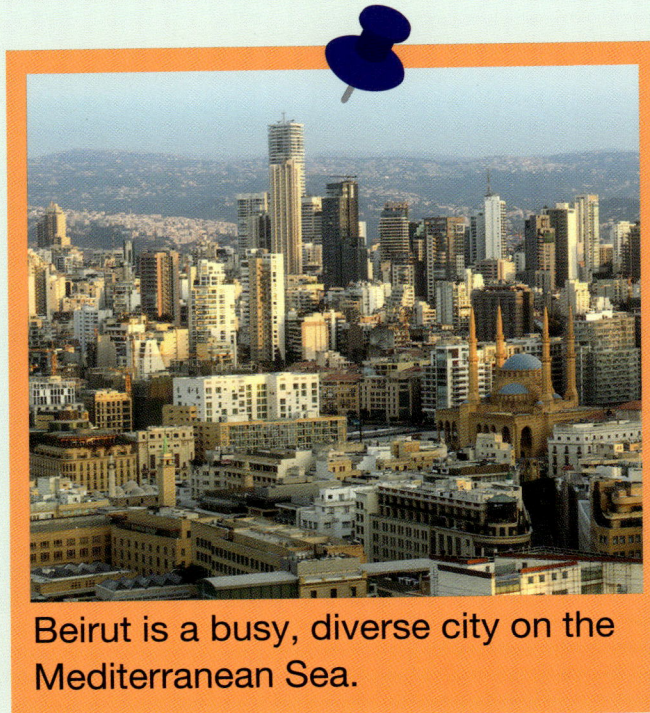

Beirut is a busy, diverse city on the Mediterranean Sea.

Records of people living in the area that is now Lebanon date back 5,000 years. Settlements in Lebanon likely existed

The cedars of Lebanon are evergreen trees that can grow up to 90 feet (27.4 meters) tall.

even before these records. Lebanon's geography, or natural features, made it a great place to settle.

Lebanon is located on the Mediterranean Sea. That made it easy to travel and trade. Past the coastal plain are the Lebanon Mountains. This mountain range runs north to south. It is parallel,

FACT!

Qurnat al-Sawdā' is Lebanon's tallest peak at more than 10,000 feet (3,048 meters) tall.

Huge cedar trees are part of Lebanon's culture. They provided wood and shade for much of Lebanon's history. Today, most trees are in **reserves** in the Lebanon Mountains.

The Litani River irrigates, or brings water to, the Bekaa Valley.

or side-by-side, with what are known as the Anti-Lebanon Mountains. This mountain range marks Lebanon's border with Syria.

Between the mountains lies the Bekaa Valley. It is very fertile, or good for farming. That's because it gets water from the mountains. More than a dozen rivers flow from the mountains, bringing water to the valley.

History

Many peoples have ruled the area that is now Lebanon. The Phoenicians were one of the first ancient **civilizations** in the area. Assyrians, Persians, Greeks,

Ancient buildings, such as this Roman temple, are found throughout Lebanon.

Romans, and Byzantines also ruled the area over time. In the 16th century, the area became part of the Ottoman Empire along with much of today's Middle East.

Lebanon was part of the Ottoman Empire until 1918. Then, France took over Lebanon for several decades. In the mid-1940s, Lebanon became an

FACT!

The Phoenicians created the first known alphabet in the world.

8

The Results of War

Middle Eastern conflicts, including Israeli-Palestinian and Syrian wars, often affect Lebanon. Because of those conflicts, nearly a million **refugees** live in Lebanon.

independent nation. Independence came with challenges, however. Both Christians and Muslims lived in Lebanon. There were many **conflicts** between them—especially when it came to ruling the new country.

Lebanon faced a **civil war** between 1975 and 1990. Christian forces fought Muslim forces. The neighboring countries of Syria and Israel got involved in the conflict, as did some Palestinians.

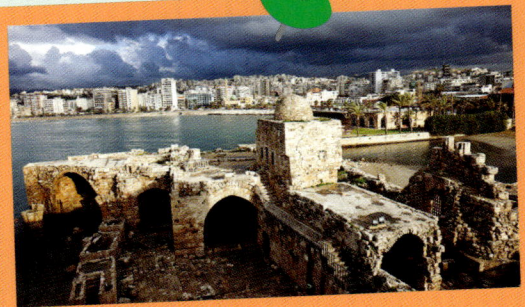

The ancient Sidon Sea Castle stands beside the modern city of Sidon, Lebanon.

VOTE ✓

Lebanon is a kind of republic. That means citizens have a voice in their government. They vote for elected officials to represent them. Parliament is the

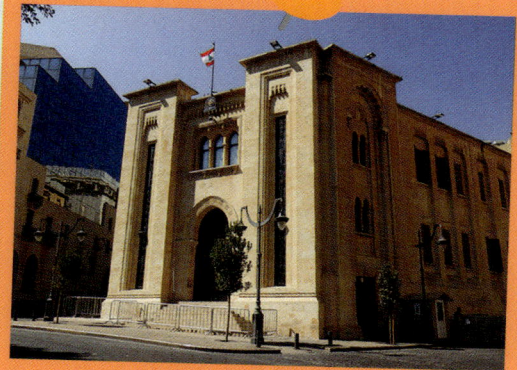

Lebanon's parliament meets in Beirut.

lawmaking body in Lebanon. The president is the head of state and has executive powers, or the ability to sign laws into effect. The prime minister chooses a cabinet of leaders who also have executive powers.

FACT!

In August 2020, countries across the world sent help to Lebanon after a deadly blast in Beirut.

Different Political Parties

Different religions often support different political parties, or groups with different ideas about how the government should be run, in Lebanon.

Today's government in Lebanon shows the effects of the civil war. Lebanon attempts to include both Christian and Muslim leaders equally in government. Each position is filled by someone of a specific religion, or belief system. The

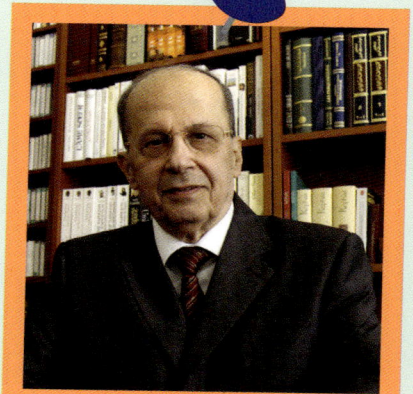

Michel Aoun was elected president of Lebanon in 2016.

president has to be Maronite Christian. The prime minister must be a Sunni Muslim. The speaker of the National Assembly must be a Shi'i (also known as Shia) Muslim.

Lebanon's location on the Mediterranean Sea made it a trade center for much of its history. Lebanese people have worked with their landscape to grow many crops. Olives, grapes, figs, and almonds are grown in the hills, while peaches, plums, apples, and pears are grown in the mountains. Vegetables and tropical fruits are grown on the coast. These crops can be sold within the country or exported, or sold to

Beirut's port is one of the major trading centers in Lebanon.

FACT!

Lebanon's unit of money is the Lebanese pound.

Lebanon buys goods from other countries. These are called imports. Lebanon imports goods from the United States, China, and European countries.

other countries. **Textiles** are other products that are manufactured, or made, in Lebanon.

Unfortunately, the civil war hurt the **infrastructure** of the country, as well as its economy—its system of making, buying, and selling goods and services. Most factories were ruined, which hurt textile manufacturing. The economy recovered for a while, but recent years have seen new problems.

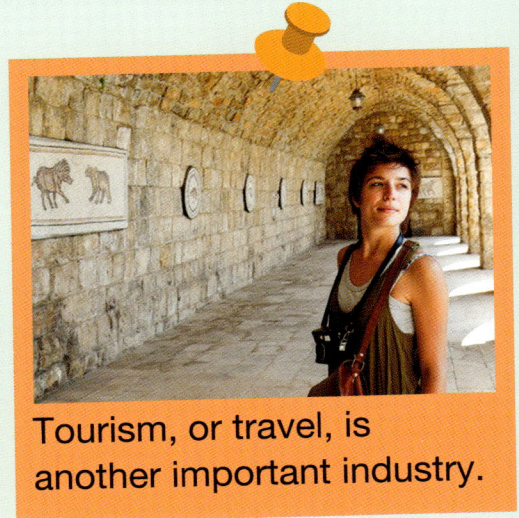

Tourism, or travel, is another important industry.

13

Lebanon's environment, or natural world, was rich for much of history. It had rivers and a fertile valley. It was home to many cedar trees. Many wild animals and plants were found in the mountains,

Loggerhead turtles (shown here) and gray wolves are endangered, or at risk of dying out.

forests, and coastal areas, from loggerhead sea turtles to gray wolves.

Today, the environment in Lebanon is very different. This is partly because the government

FACT!

Water birds such as flamingos, pelicans, and herons are found in the marshes of Lebanon.

let businesses cut down too many trees for wood. Now, native plants are unable to grow in many places. There are more low trees and brush than before. Hot, dry weather due to climate change—change in Earth's weather caused by people—leads to wildfires. Farms and factories pollute the water and air.

Beirut is sometimes covered in a thick layer of smog, or smoke and air pollution.

Hope for the Future

Environmental groups hope to save Lebanon's environment from waste, pollution, and overuse of **resources.** They fight for laws to keep the environment from harm.

The People Today

Lebanon is a diverse country. There are different **ethnic** and religious groups living all in one place. That's because trade and changing empires brought many people through the area. Arabs make up the largest ethnic group in Lebanon. Many Christians in Lebanon identify as Phoenicians, or **descendants** of the early peoples who first settled

Kids go to school at this refugee camp in Lebanon.

FACT!

In Lebanon, the life expectancy, or number of years someone is expected to live on average, is 78.

in Lebanon. Smaller ethnic groups in Lebanon include Armenians, Greeks, and Kurds.

Lebanon has a population of around 6.8 million people. Around a million people are refugees. Refugees have come from Palestine, Iraq, and Syria. In recent years, the number of Syrian refugees has increased as the civil war in Syria rages on. Refugees leave their homes when their lives are in danger.

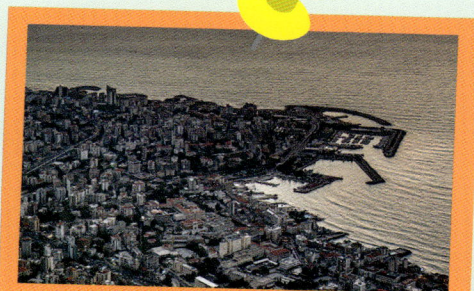

Today, most people live on the Mediterranean coast of Lebanon.

Beirut Today

Beirut is the biggest city in Lebanon. About 2 million people live in and around it. People of many ethnicities and religions live together in Beirut.

Lifestyle

Urbanization, or an increase in and greater movement to cities, has greatly changed the lifestyle in Lebanon. Today, most people live in cities. People in cities get around by bus, car, taxi, or foot. Cities have workplaces, factories, and busy ports, as well as restaurants, museums, and hotels.

This Lebanese woman wears a hijab on her head.

Family life is different across different ethnic and religious groups. However, in most cases, families are very important to the Lebanese

FACT!

A 2017 poll found that Lebanon had the best opportunities for women in the workplace of all MENA (Middle East and North Africa) countries.

lifestyle. People are often expected to honor their family and respect their elders. Many extended families live near one another. Many still follow traditional family roles, or parts. The father is often seen as the head of the house, while the mother takes care of the household. Still, many Lebanese women go to college and work outside the household.

Lebanese families love to share a meal together.

Women in Islamic Communities

Some Muslim women are expected to dress a certain way. Some wear cloaks called abayas and cover their hair with hijabs.

Religion

Religion is very important in Lebanon. Different religious groups practice and live side by side in cities. However, in some places, religion separates people into different communities. Religious differences have also led to conflict.

The Mohammad Al-Amin Mosque and St. George Maronite Cathedral stand side by side in Lebanon.

Islam has more followers than any other religion in Lebanon. People who follow Islam are called Muslims. Islam has been around since the seventh century AD. Muslims believe an angel named Gabriel revealed, or told, the words of

FACT!

Lebanon has 17 official religions.

Major Muslim holidays include Eid al-Fitr and Eid al-Adha. Christian holidays include Easter, Christmas, and St. Maron's Day.

Allah (God) to the **Prophet** Muhammad. Their main holy text is the Quran. Two sects, or divisions, of Islam are Sunni and Shia. Both Sunni and Shia Islam are practiced in Lebanon.

Muslims pray five times a day facing the direction of Mecca in Saudi Arabia.

Christianity is also practiced in Lebanon. Christians believe that Jesus Christ is the son of God and follow his teachings. Most Christians in Lebanon are Maronite. That is an Arab sect of the Catholic Church—a branch of Christianity.

21

Language

The main language people speak in Lebanon is Arabic. It is the national language of Lebanon. Arabic is the main language spoken in most Arab League countries. It's the language of Islam, as the Quran is written in Arabic.

People read Arabic from right to left, rather than left to right.

Fusha is the classical form of Arabic found in the Quran and formal texts. Modern Standard Arabic is used in many modern written works.

FACT!

More than 300 million people around the world speak Arabic.

The Arab League

The Arab League was founded in 1945. It's a group of 22 Arab countries who work together on matters of common interest.

Ammiya is the everyday form of Arabic people use when they talk to one another.

Some signs in Lebanon have two languages on them.

Many people in Lebanon also speak French because of the country's history as a French colony. Today, many younger people speak English too. Some people are concerned that younger people are starting to favor English instead of Arabic in Lebanon. These people want to keep the long history of speaking Arabic in Lebanon alive.

Arts and Festivals

Beirut was once an international center for the arts. However, the arts suffered during the civil war. Today, the arts are once again taking hold in Lebanon. Lebanese arts are a mix of traditional and modern styles.

Lebanese singer Majida El Roumi sings at the Beiteddine Arts Festival.

People make music using hand drums, stringed instruments such as lutes, and a type of double clarinet called a *mijwiz*. The national dance is the *dabke*. One popular form of dabke involves people

FACT!

The Beiteddine Arts Festival is a three-month celebration of Lebanese art, drama, and music.

Lebanese Independence Day is celebrated on November 22. It marks the day that Lebanon gained its freedom from France. People enjoy parades and celebrations of Lebanese culture.

dancing in a big group, in a circle or line. Lebanese people often dance this dabke at weddings.

Music festivals include the Byblos Festival, Zouk Mikael International Festival, and Baalbeck International Festival. The Baalbeck International Festival takes place in the Roman ruins of Baalbeck. The Tyre and South Festival celebrates the dances, poetry, music, and crafts of southern Lebanon.

Caracalla Dance Theatre performs at the Baalbeck International Festival.

25

Lebanon has both snow-topped mountains and sandy beaches. That makes for exciting, diverse outdoor activities in the country. People in Lebanon can swim and ski in the same

Fans cheer for Lebanon during a basketball game.

day! People can visit ski resorts in the Lebanon Mountains for snow sports. They can also hike and bike through the mountains. Other people enjoy water sports, such as kayaking and windsurfing, on the coast.

FACT!

Lebanon hosted the Asian Cup, a major soccer competition, in 2000.

People can connect with nature at parks and reserves in Lebanon. Reserves include the Shouf Cedars Reserve, Jabal Moussa Biosphere Reserve, and the Cedars of God.

Lebanon's snowy peaks and sunny weather are perfect for skiing.

Soccer is one of the most popular sports in Lebanon. In most of the world, including Lebanon, it's called football. Professional players are part of the Lebanese Football Association. People in Lebanon also enjoy basketball. It's a simple game that doesn't need more than a ball and basket, so it can be played nearly anywhere by anyone.

Food

Gathering for meals is important for families and communities. Many Lebanese foods are similar to foods in other Middle Eastern and Mediterranean countries.

Hummus usually combines chickpeas, oils, tahini (sesame paste), and garlic.

Probably the most well-known Lebanese food is hummus. Made from chickpeas, this spread can be eaten with a flatbread called pita. Chickpeas are also shaped into a ball in a dish called falafel. A dish called tabbouleh combines a grain called

FACT!

Ma'amoul is a Lebanese cookie filled with fruits and nuts.

Perfect Pita

Pita is also known as "pocket bread." It can hold meats and spreads. It is similar to flatbreads eaten in other Arabic countries. It has been eaten for thousands of years.

bulgur wheat with herbs such as mint and parsley. Fattoush is a healthy vegetable dish also eaten with pita.

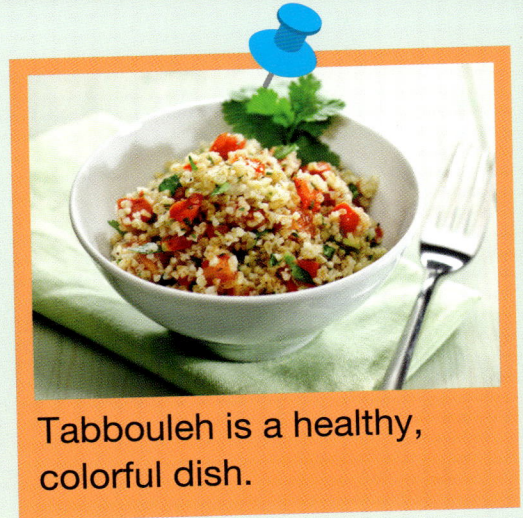

Tabbouleh is a healthy, colorful dish.

Lamb is a popular meat in Lebanon. People often eat an open-faced meat pie called *sfiha*. Lebanese people often cook meats such as lamb or chicken slowly on a skewer, or stick, for shawarma. As with much of Lebanese culture, many foods are a mix of the old and new!

Glossary

civilization   An organized society with written records and laws.

civil war   A war between two opposing groups within a country.

complex   Having many parts.

conflict   A fight, battle, or war.

descendant   Someone related to a person or group of people who lived at an earlier time.

diverse   Different or varied.

ethnic   Of or relating to large groups of people who have the same cultural background and ways of life.

infrastructure   The basic equipment and structures (such as roads and bridges) that are needed for a country, region, or organization to function properly.

prophet   Someone who delivers messages that are believed to have come from God.

refugee   Someone who has to leave their home country, especially during a time of war.

reserve   A place where something is kept safe from harm.

resource   Something that can be used.

textile   A kind of cloth that is woven or knit.

tradition   Something that's been done for a long time.

Find Out More

Books

Brundle, Harriet. *Refugees*. King's Lynn, Norfolk, UK: The Secret Book Company, 2018.

Persano, Thomas. *Lebanon*. New York, NY: Bearport Publishing, 2019.

Website

Lebanon Facts for Kids

kids.kiddle.co/Lebanon

Discover more facts about Lebanon.

Video

Lebanon—Geography for Kids

www.youtube.com/watch?v=1C3GH34kz_w

Explore the geography of Lebanon.

Index

About the Author

Menna Landon is a world traveler and author who once lived in a tree house. Her one regret is that she can't bring her cat on her adventures. It's not you, Leo, it's the airline industry.